Kids' UKULELE Songbook

BY ✈ EMILY → ARROW

T0016650

_____'s
write your name

UKULELE SONGBOOK

Kids' URULELE Songbook

BY ⇨EMILY⇨ ARROW

PHOTOGRAPHY BY ALEX CRAWFORD

Learn **30** Songs to Sing and Play

Happy Fox BOOKS

Color in page 1 and write your name to make this book your own!

ISBN 978-1-64124-148-9

Project Team
Editor: Colleen Dorsey
Cover design: Llara Pazdan
Interior page design: Llara Pazdan
Indexer: Jay Kreider

Library of Congress Control Number: 2021945350

To learn more about the other great books from Fox Chapel Publishing, or to find a retailer near you, call toll-free 800-457-9112 or visit us at *www.FoxChapelPublishing.com*.

We are always looking for talented authors. To submit an idea, please send a brief inquiry to acquisitions@foxchapelpublishing.com.

Fox Chapel Publishing makes every effort to use environmentally friendly paper for printing.

Printed in China
First printing

Image Credits
All author photography by Alex Crawford.
The following graphics throughout are credited to Freepik (Designed by Freepik): Repeat Rainbow graphic; Practice Journey ukulele graphic; Rockstar Ending graphic
The following images are credited to Shutterstock.com and their respective creators: illustrations (1, 6): Sono Ringo; boy (1): New Africa; girl (7): S_Sukpon; islands (10): ShEd Artworks; ukulele (11): Istry Istry; girl (12): Roman Chazov; smartphone (13): Nikola Stanisic; sandwich (26): summer studio; girl (27): Vasin Lee; girls (29): February_Love; weather icons (36–38): Eugenia Petrovskaya; kids (41): Rawpixel.com; moon (43): Mr. Turgut Birgin; dog (44): Ezzolo; letters (46): mhatzapa; bus (50): petite lili; girl (59): Yuganov Konstantin; kids (61): Rawpixel.com; girl (63): Waraphorn Aphai; pizza graphics (66–67): primiaou; llama (72): Anastasia Trapeznikova; food graphics (75): Drawlab19; bear (76): babachock; boy (79): AnnGaysorn; kid (85): Evgeny Atamanenko; kids (87): Ronnachai Palas; top boy (88): Volurol; bottom boy (88): BAZA Production; girl (89): Inside Creative House; boy (89): sportoakimirka; kids (92): gpointstudio; kids (94): Rawpixel.com; squiggly lines and hash marks (throughout): Krolja; bursts (throughout): Fourleaflover; music notes (throughout): mhatzapa; watercolor elements (throughout): samui; Practice & Shine Chart background (throughout): Tonktiti; blue-green background (ex. 11, throughout): Aepsilon

Hello! Hello!

I'm Emily Arrow, and I love to play and teach ukulele. With my ukulele, I write songs and create videos to share with listeners around the world. And I have a very special way of teaching music . . . *the Arrow way!*

The ukulele is a special instrument to many people, and for many reasons. One reason I love the ukulele is that I can bring it with me wherever I go! That means I can practice ukulele outdoors and on my porch. And I can bring my ukulele to bookstores, parks, and cafes where I can share ukulele songs with others. And the most magical reason I love the ukulele is that playing music makes me feel calm and helps me learn more about myself.

Are you ready to play ukulele together? This songbook will help you sing and play *the Arrow way!*

THIS SONGBOOK WILL EXPLORE:

- a quick-start guide to tuning
- 8 colorful chords
- 5 strumming patterns
- fingerpicking
- melodies on the frets
- and songwriting!

If you haven't already checked out my first book, *Kids' Guide to Learning the Ukulele*, that book goes into much more detail about learning to play the ukulele and features different songs. But if you haven't, don't worry—you'll still learn the basics in this book and be able to play all this book's songs!

Table of Contents

30 Songs to Learn & Play

Getting STARTED

In this section you'll learn:

🎸 All about the ukulele

🎸 How to tune your ukulele

🎸 The 8 colorful chords you'll play

🎸 Different ways to strum

About the UKULELE

The instrument we now know as the **ukulele** was inspired by an instrument called the **machete**. The machete was introduced to the Islands of Hawaii by Portugese immigrants in the 1800's and looked very similar to a guitar before it became the ukulele. Now, the ukulele is a widely celebrated musical instrument in the Hawaiian Islands . . . and beyond!

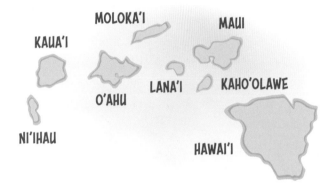

KAUA'I

MOLOKA'I

MAUI

LANA'I

KAHO'OLAWE

O'AHU

NI'IHAU

HAWAI'I

Did you know that the Hawaiian Queen Lili'uokalani played the ukulele? Queen Lili'uokalani was a songwriter, and she wrote the song **"Aloha 'Oe"** as well as many other songs.

I love learning about the ukulele and the many musicians who play this special instrument. Let's practice pronouncing, or speaking, the word *ukulele*. In the Hawaiian language, the word "ukulele" means "jumping flea," because the sound of the strings is light and playful like a flea is hopping on them! The word ukulele is pronounced like this: **oo-koo-lay-lay.**

oo-koo-lay-lay

When I'm practicing my ukulele, I think it's fun to open a songbook and learn a new song or even write my own! So in this book, you can learn, practice, and write songs on your own ukulele.

Ready to strum along?

Holding Your Ukulele

First, imagine your ukulele is a puppet with a body, neck, head, and even a mouth!

Sit on the edge of a chair or on the floor with your back comfortably straight.

With your <u>left hand</u>, hold the ukulele's **neck** below the **head** (where the tuning **pegs** are).

With your <u>right arm</u>, hold the ukulele's body so your right hand can still reach the strings to strum. Your right hand will strum over the **sound hole**, the circle-shaped opening where the sound vibrates out from.

What to do if you're left-handed: Guess what? I'm left-handed! And I still play the ukulele by holding the neck with my left hand and strumming with my right hand. If you're left-handed too, I find it helpful to still learn this way even if it feels "backwards" at first.

Parts of the Ukulele

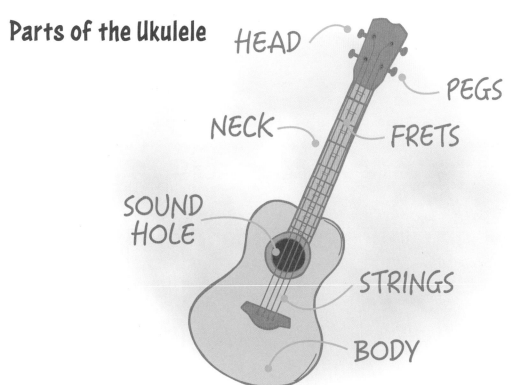

HEAD

PEGS

NECK

FRETS

SOUND HOLE

STRINGS

BODY

Tuning and Strumming

Tuning

The ukulele strings are numbered 4, 3, 2, and 1 from the top string (4) to the bottom string (1). When you're holding your ukulele (with the neck to your left side), string 4 is closest to your chin.

Each string number has a **musical pitch**, or letter name. The string's musical pitches are G, C, E, and A.

> String 4 is the musical pitch G
>
> String 3 is the musical pitch C
>
> String 2 is the musical pitch E
>
> String 1 is the musical pitch A

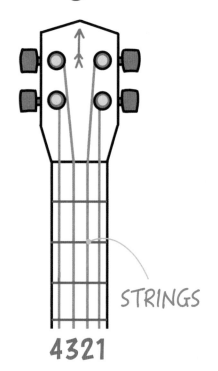

STRINGS

4321

Here's a funny way to remember each string's letter names for tuning: Good Cats Eat Apples.

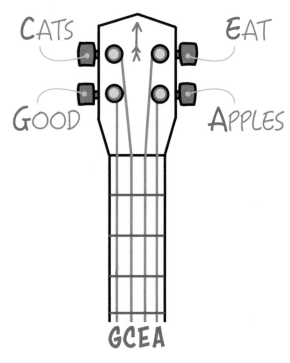

CATS

EAT

GOOD

APPLES

GCEA

The simplest way to tune is with an electronic tuning device or app. To tune your ukulele, twist each string using the **tuning pegs** until the string matches the musical pitch it's supposed to be.

Beginning with the G string, turn the string's tuning peg while your **right hand** plucks the string aloud. Turn until the tuner lets you know the string's musical pitch is correct.

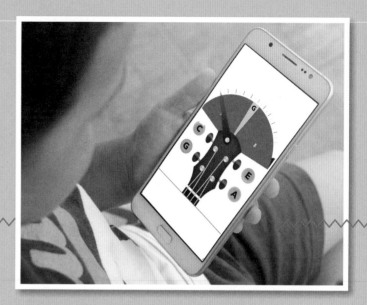

WHICH DIRECTION TO TWIST:

For strings G and C, twist *to the sky* to make it sound high! *(twist left or counter-clockwise)*

For strings E and A, twist *to the ground* to make a high sound! *(twist right or clockwise)*

Strumming

There are many ways to strum an instrument with strings. Here are two of my favorite options: **pinch strum** and **thumb strum**. Try each one on the open strings to see what feels the best to you.

Pinch Strum

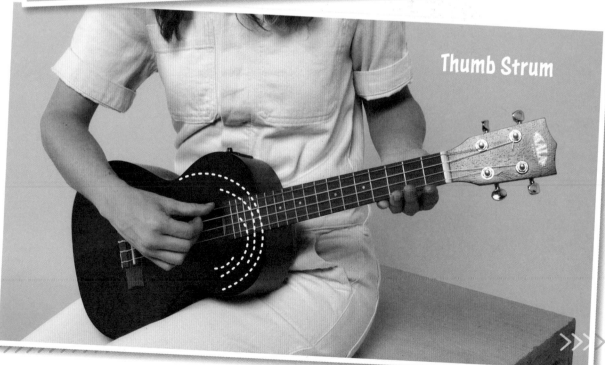

Thumb Strum

DOWN STRUM

When you see the **down strum** arrows ↓, your <u>right hand</u> will strum downward through all of the strings together. A **down strum** goes from the top **G** string to the bottom **A** string. Sing or speak the below words to your own tune.

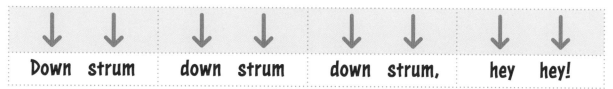

↓	↓	↓	↓	↓	↓	↓	↓
Down	strum	down	strum	down	strum,	hey	hey!

PATTING

When you see this symbol, pat the strings over the sound hole with your right hand. This will stop the sound and make a light pat sound to keep the beat.

The 8 Colorful Chords

Chords are played by pressing down on the strings with your <u>left hand</u> on specific frets on the neck of the ukulele. In this songbook, each of the 8 chords will have a color to help you remember the chord letter names and shapes.

Frets are the lines on the neck of the ukulele that look like boxes or rows. The 1st fret is the line closest to the head of the ukulele. To make a chord shape, press down just above the fret with a curled, firm finger.

GCEA

1st fret
2nd fret
3rd fret
4th fret

The **finger numbers** on your left hand are labeled 1, 2, and 3, starting at your pointer finger.

1 2 3

8 Colorful Chords to Practice and Play

 **C CHORD**

In this songbook, the C Chord is like our home base. We'll start and end many songs on C and will play this chord in almost every song, so it's a great place to begin!

To play the C Chord, press down on the 3rd fret of the A string (bottom string) with *finger 3* of your left hand.

Remember: Your finger will be in between the second and third fret, not ON the fret.

FRET	STRING	FINGER
3rd fret	A string	3rd finger

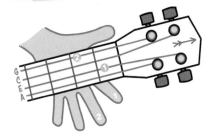

 **F CHORD**

The F Chord uses fingers 1 and 2, or your "bunny ear fingers."

To play the F Chord, press down on the 2nd fret of the G string (top string) with *finger 2* and on the 1st fret of the E string with *finger 1.*

FRET	STRING	FINGER
2nd fret	G string	2nd finger
1st fret	E string	1st finger

G CHORD

For the G Chord, you'll need three fingers. So begin by placing your "bunny ear fingers," fingers 1 and 2, where they belong. Then add finger 3. G is a challenging chord, so remember to treat yourself kindly while you practice.

To play the G Chord, press down on the 2nd fret of the C string with *finger 1* and the 2nd fret of the A string with *finger 2.* Then press down on the 3rd fret of the E string with *finger 3.*

FRET	STRING	FINGER
2nd fret	C string	1st finger
2nd fret	A string	2nd finger
3rd fret	E string	3rd finger

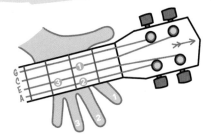

A MINOR CHORD

The A Minor Chord (Am) may sound more warm or emotional because it's a minor chord. **Minor chords** have a combination of notes that may sound more sad or blue than other chords. Listen while you play the Am Chord to notice what sounds different about minor chords to you!

To play the Am Chord, press down on the 2nd fret of the G string with *finger 2*.

FRET	STRING	FINGER
2nd fret	G string	2nd finger

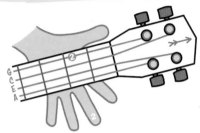

D MINOR CHORD

Similar to the Am Chord, the D Minor Chord (Dm) may sound more warm or emotional because it's a minor chord. Dm is played with three fingers, so be patient with your fingers while you're learning where each finger goes.

To play the Dm Chord, press down on the 2nd fret of the G string with *finger 2* and the 2nd fret of the C string with *finger 3*. Then press down on the 1st fret of the E string with *finger 1*.

FRET	STRING	FINGER
2nd fret	G string	2nd finger
2nd fret	C string	3rd finger
1st fret	E string	1st finger

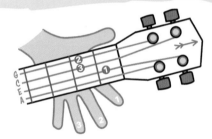

7 CHORDS

7 chords may sound playful and energetic. My nickname for 7 chords is "sparkle chords" because they have extra pizzazz! The 7 chords in this songbook are:

 **C7 CHORD**

The C7 Chord is similar to the C Chord because it's played on the same string, just on a higher fret.

To play the C7 Chord, press down on the 1st fret of the A string with *finger 1*.

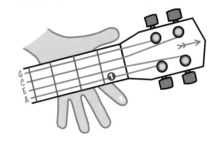

FRET	STRING	FINGER
1st fret	A string	1st finger

 G7 CHORD

To learn the G7 Chord, it helps to imagine that G7 is a reversed, or upside-down, version of the G Chord.

To play the G7 Chord, press down on the 1st fret of the E string with *finger 1*. Then press the 2nd fret of the C string with *finger 2* and the 2nd fret of the A string with *finger 3*.

FRET	STRING	FINGER
1st fret	E string	1st finger
2nd fret	C string	2nd finger
2nd fret	A string	3rd finger

 A7 CHORD

Since the A7 Chord is a 7 chord, or what I call a "sparkle chord," it may sound more playful and energetic. It helps to remember that both the A7 Chord and the Am Chord are single-finger chord shapes.

To play the A7 Chord, press down on the 1st fret of the C string with *finger 1*.

FRET	STRING	FINGER
1st fret	C string	1st finger

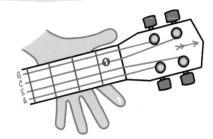

Strumming Patterns

5 Strumming Arrows

This songbook will use 5 different types of strums, written as arrows.

DOWN
one down strum

DOWN-DOWN
two quick down strums

DOWN-UP
start down, then strum *back up* through all of the string

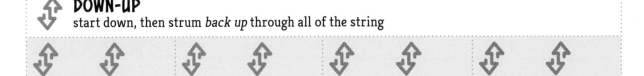

UP-DOWN
start up, then strum *back down* through all of the strings; not as common as the others, often paired with a down-down

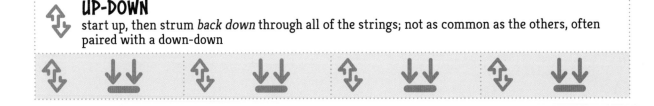

WHOLE DOWN
hold a down strum for the *whole beat*; it helps to strum and then think: *wait*

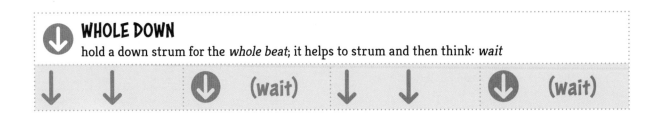

Practice Strumming Patterns

Try these strumming arrows in different **strumming patterns**. You can choose a chord shape to play with your left hand or just play the open strings. Draw a star ☆ in the box next to the patterns you've tried so far!

1.

DOWN	DOWN	DOWN	DOWN	DOWN	DOWN	DOWN	DOWN
↓	↓	↓	↓	↓	↓	↓	↓

☐

2.

DOWN	DOWN	DOWN-DOWN	DOWN	DOWN	DOWN	DOWN-DOWN	DOWN
↓	↓	↓↓	↓	↓	↓	↓↓	↓

☐

3.

DOWN	DOWN	DOWN-UP	DOWN	DOWN	DOWN	DOWN-UP	DOWN
↓	↓	↕	↓	↓	↓	↕	↓

☐

4.

DOWN-DOWN	UP-DOWN	DOWN-DOWN	UP-DOWN	DOWN-DOWN	UP-DOWN	DOWN-DOWN	UP-DOWN
↓↓	↕	↓↓	↕	↓↓	↕	↓↓	↕

☐

5.

DOWN	DOWN	WHOLE DOWN	DOWN	DOWN	WHOLE DOWN
↓	↓	⬇ (wait)	↓	↓	⬇ (wait)

☐

30 Songs
to Learn
& Play

How to sing the songs
while you strum:

🎸 sing the tune if
you know it

or

🎸 create your own way
of singing the words

or

🎸 speak the words

or

🎸 any combination of
singing and speaking

LISTEN FIRST!
To listen and strum
along to some of these songs, visit
www.emilyarrow.com/ukulelesongs

The First Song Ever

BY EMILY ARROW

CHORDS: 0 = OPEN STRINGS

Welcome to the first song ever! Well, the first song ever . . . *in this book.* 😆 For "The First Song Ever," your <u>right hand</u> will strum through all of the strings together. Your <u>left hand</u> will play **open strings** (0). **Open strings** means your left hand won't need to press down on any of the strings on the neck.

Can you find the spots in the song where the strumming arrows switch from **down strums** ↓ to **down-down strums** ↓↓? Sing along to the lyrics in your own way!

SINGALONG							
↓	↓	↓	↓	↓↓	↓↓	↓↓	↓
It's	the	first	song	ev-er	ev-er	ev-er	hey!
↓	↓	↓	↓	↓↓	↓↓	↓	↓
Play	the	first	song	ev-er	ev-er	all	day!

PRACTICE & SHINE CHART

At the bottom of each song, keep track of your practicing until you feel ready to shine! Draw a checkmark, star, or any shape of your choice in the boxes.

FIRST TRY	THREE MORE TIMES	READY TO SHINE!
☆	☆ ☆ ☆	☆
First Try: When you play a song for the first time, check off the first box	**Three More Times:** *Three* boxes for three different times you review the song	**Ready to Shine:** Keep practicing until you feel like the song is smooth, shareable, and ready to shine!

The 2 Chord Sandwich Song

BY EMILY ARROW

CHORDS: C, F

Switching between two chords can be challenging. This song will help your fingers learn to switch quickly between  C and F. Sing along to the lyrics in your own way!

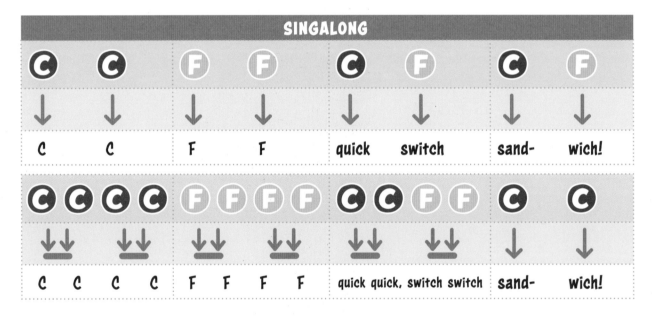

SINGALONG							
C	C	F	F	C	F	C	F
↓	↓	↓	↓	↓	↓	↓	↓
C	C	F	F	quick	switch	sand-	wich!

C C	C C	F F	F F	C C	F F	C	C
↓↓	↓↓	↓↓	↓↓	↓↓	↓↓	↓	↓
C C	C C	F F	F F	quick quick,	switch switch	sand-	wich!

PRACTICE & SHINE CHART

Draw a checkmark, star, or any shape of your choice in the boxes.

FIRST TRY	THREE MORE TIMES			READY TO SHINE!
☐	☐	☐	☐	☐

The 4 Chord Song

BY EMILY ARROW
CHORDS: FIGURE IT OUT BELOW!

Try this song to earn the 4 Chord Friend patch! One you've gotten to "Ready to Shine!" on your Practice & Shine Chart, color in the patch to celebrate your hard work learning four chords. Sing along to the lyrics in your own way!

What are the 4 different chords in this song?

_____   _____   _____   _____

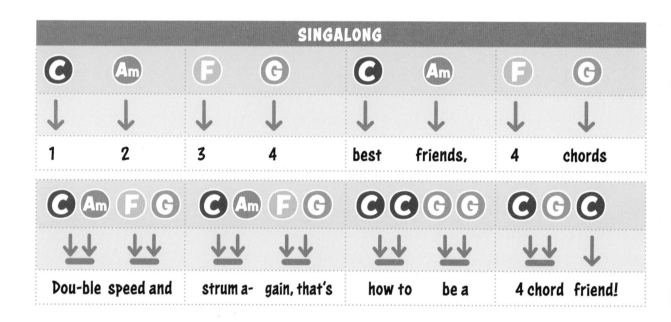

SINGALONG							
C	Am	F	G	C	Am	F	G
↓	↓	↓	↓	↓	↓	↓	↓
1	2	3	4	best	friends,	4	chords

C Am F G	C Am F G	C C G G	C G C
↓↓ ↓↓	↓↓ ↓↓	↓↓ ↓↓	↓↓ ↓
Dou-ble speed and	strum a- gain, that's	how to be a	4 chord friend!

PRACTICE & SHINE CHART

Draw a checkmark, star, or any shape of your choice in the boxes.

FIRST TRY	THREE MORE TIMES	READY TO SHINE!
☐	☐ ☐ ☐	☐

The 8 Chord Song

BY EMILY ARROW
CHORDS: FIGURE IT OUT BELOW!

Now, try this song to earn the 8 Chord Friend patch!
One you've gotten to "Ready to Shine!" on your Practice
& Shine Chart, color in the patch to celebrate your hard
work learning 8 chords.

What are the 8 different chords in this song?

_____ _____ _____ _____

_____ _____ _____ _____

This song has two parts: a **verse** and a **chorus**. Usually the **verse** part of a song tells the details of the song's story. The verse lyrics are usually unique each time you sing the verse. The lyrics of the **chorus** are usually the same every time you repeat them.

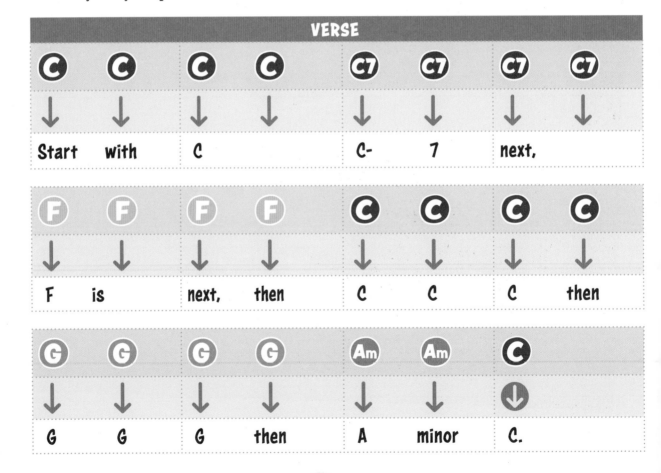

VERSE							
C	C	C	C	C7	C7	C7	C7
↓	↓	↓	↓	↓	↓	↓	↓
Start	with	C		C-	7	next,	
F	F	F	F	C	C	C	C
↓	↓	↓	↓	↓	↓	↓	↓
F	is	next,	then	C	C	C	then
G	G	G	G	Am	Am	C	
↓	↓	↓	↓	↓	↓	⬇	
G	G	G	then	A	minor	C.	

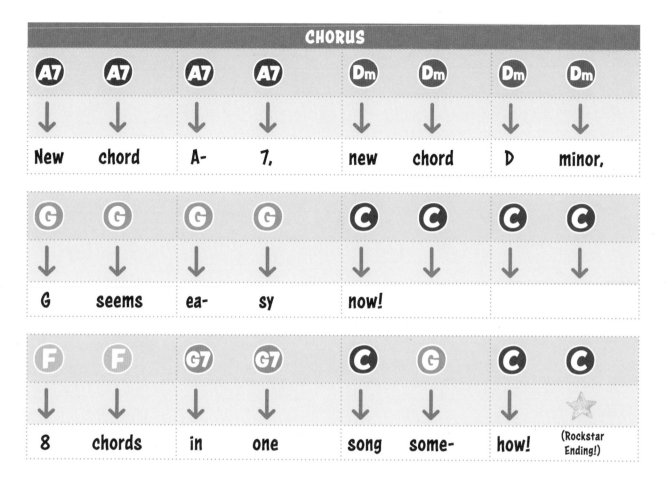

CHORUS

A7	A7	A7	A7	Dm	Dm	Dm	Dm
↓	↓	↓	↓	↓	↓	↓	↓
New	chord	A-	7,	new	chord	D	minor,

G	G	G	G	C	C	C	C
↓	↓	↓	↓	↓	↓	↓	↓
G	seems	ea-	sy	now!			

F	F	G7	G7	C	G	C	C
↓	↓	↓	↓	↓	↓	↓	☆
8	chords	in	one	song	some-	how!	(Rockstar Ending!)

When you see a ☆ in this book at the end of a song, it means play a **rockstar ending**! A rockstar ending is when you play the last chord many times quickly with a down-up ↕ strum to celebrate the end of the song . . . like a rockstar!

PRACTICE & SHINE CHART

Draw a checkmark, star, or any shape of your choice in the boxes.

FIRST TRY	THREE MORE TIMES	READY TO SHINE!
☐	☐ ☐ ☐	☐

Repeat Rainbow Song

BY EMILY ARROW
CHORDS: F, C, G7, C7

In this songbook, when you see the **repeat rainbow**  it means to repeat the song. To **repeat** means to play it again. Sing along to the lyrics in your own way!

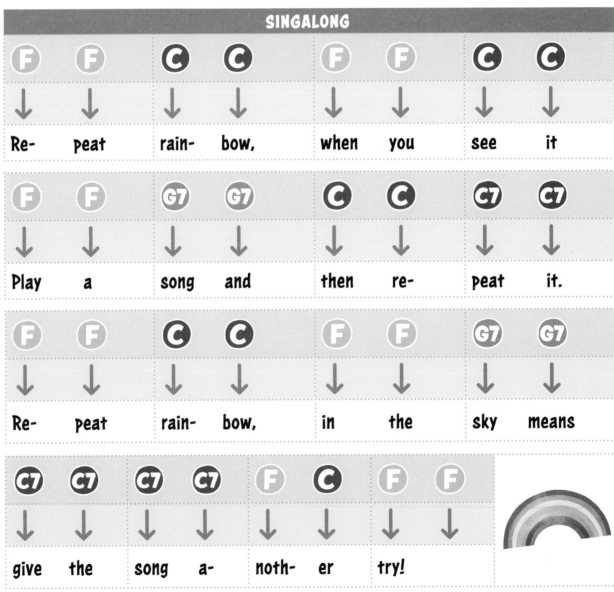

SINGALONG

F	F	C	C	F	F	C	C
↓	↓	↓	↓	↓	↓	↓	↓
Re-	peat	rain-	bow,	when	you	see	it

F	F	G7	G7	C	C	C7	C7
↓	↓	↓	↓	↓	↓	↓	↓
Play	a	song	and	then	re-	peat	it.

F	F	C	C	F	F	G7	G7
↓	↓	↓	↓	↓	↓	↓	↓
Re-	peat	rain-	bow,	in	the	sky	means

C7	C7	C7	C7	F	C	F	F
↓	↓	↓	↓	↓	↓	↓	↓
give	the	song	a-	noth-	er	try!	

PRACTICE & SHINE CHART

Draw a checkmark, star, or any shape of your choice in the boxes.

FIRST TRY	THREE MORE TIMES	READY TO SHINE!
☐	☐ ☐ ☐	☐

Hello Hello

BY EMILY ARROW
CHORDS: C, F, G

Let's sing a hello song together! Add your own name to introduce yourself, then sing through the other verse lyrics.

The song starts with 3 strums each box and then changes to 2 strums per box for the rest of the song!

LISTEN FIRST!
To listen and strum along to this song, visit www.emilyarrow.com/ukulelesongs

1	2	3	1	2	1	2	1	2
			SINGALONG					
C	C	C	C	C	C	C	F	F
↓	↓	↓	↓	↓	↓	↓	↓	↓
1. He-	llo,	he-	llo,		he-	llo	(sing your name)	
2. He-	llo,	he-	llo,		and	good	mor-	ning,
3. He-	llo,	he-	llo,		and	good	aft-	er-
4. He-	llo,	he-	llo,		he-	llo	how	are

G	G	C	C	F	F	C	
↓	↓	↓	↓	↓	↓	↓	☆
Oh,	he-	llo!					
friends,	he-	llo!					
noon,	he-	llo!					
you?	he-	llo!					

PRACTICE & SHINE CHART

Draw a checkmark, star, or any shape of your choice in the boxes.

FIRST TRY	THREE MORE TIMES	READY TO SHINE!
☐	☐ ☐ ☐	☐

How's the Weather?

BY EMILY ARROW
CHORDS: C, F, G7, G, Dm, Am

If feelings were like weather, what would each type of weather be? Maybe feeling sunny would mean you feel excited, and perhaps feeling windy might mean you feel worried. We can feel different emotions during each day, just like the weather can change from sunny to rainy. In this song, let's check in with our emotions and see if we can match them with the weather we're feeling.

   "How's the Weather?" is a **Question and Choice song**. That means, you start the song by singing the **question**. Then in the next part of the song, make a **choice** to share how you are feeling. Try singing through all of the moods and emotions, maybe even matching your singing voice to the emotions!

QUESTION

C	C	C	👋	F	F	F	👋
↓	↓	↕	✕	↓	↓	↕	✕
How's	the	wea-ther? (pat!)		How's	the	wea-ther? (pat!)	

C	C	F	F	G7	G7	C	👋
↓	↓	↕	↕	↓	↓	↓	✕
How's	the	wea-ther on the		in-		side?	(pat!)

CHOICE

Choose how you're feeling from the ideas below or write your own. Just like weather, we can have more than one feeling at the same time. Repeat the question and try making a choice again!

I feel peaceful and calm right now.

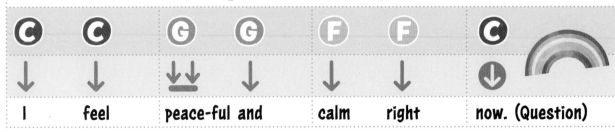

C	C	G	G	F	F	C	🌈
↓	↓	↓↓	↓	↓	↓	↓	
I	feel	peace-ful and		calm	right	now. (Question)	

I feel blue and rainy right now.

Dm	Dm	Am	Am	Am	Dm	Am
↓	↓	↓	↓	↓↓	↓	↓
I	feel	blue	and	rain-y	right	now. (Question)

I feel sunny and bright right now.

F	F	F	F	G7	G7	C
↓	↓	↓↓	↓↓	↓	↓	↓
I	feel	sun-ny	and	bright	right	now. (Question)

I feel windy and worried right now.

C	C	F	F	Am	Am	C
↓	↓	↓↓	↓	↓↓	↓	↓
I	feel	wind-y	and	worr-ied	right	now. (Question)

continued on next page

I feel thunder and frustrated now.

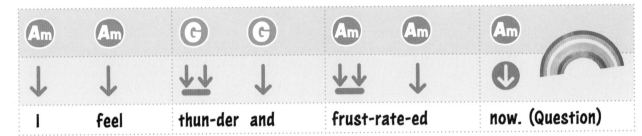

Am	Am	G	G	Am	Am	Am
↓	↓	↓↓	↓	↓↓	↓	↓
I	feel	thun-der	and	frust-rate-ed		now. (Question)

I feel a mix of weather right now.

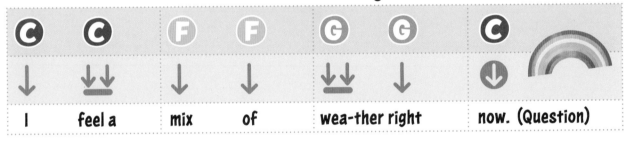

C	C	F	F	G	G	C
↓	↓↓	↓	↓	↓↓	↓	↓
I	feel a	mix	of	wea-ther right		now. (Question)

I feel _____ and _____ right now.

C	C	F	F	G	G	C
↓	↓	↓	↓	↓	↓	↓
I	feel	_____	and	_____	right	now. (Question)

PRACTICE & SHINE CHART

Draw a checkmark, star, or any shape of your choice in the boxes.

FIRST TRY	THREE MORE TIMES	READY TO SHINE!
☐	☐ ☐ ☐	☐

Sally Goes Round the Sun

CANADIAN CHILDREN'S SONG

CHORDS: C, A7, F, G

Try playing this song standing up so you can jump when you shout "BOOM!" at the end!

How to play the song as a game with others: While you sing and strum the song, everyone will walk around in a circle, jumping at the spots where you pat your ukulele. Then, at the end of the song when you shout, "BOOM," everyone will switch walking directions and the circle will walk the opposite way this time.

PATTERN PRACTICE

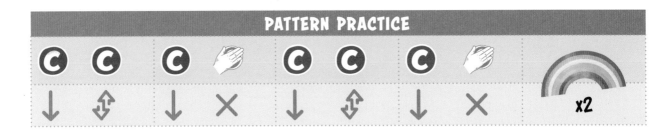

SINGALONG

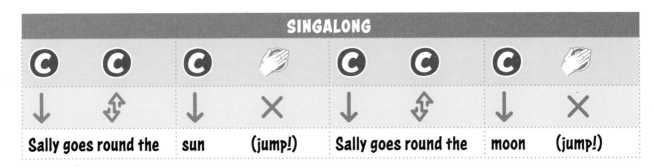

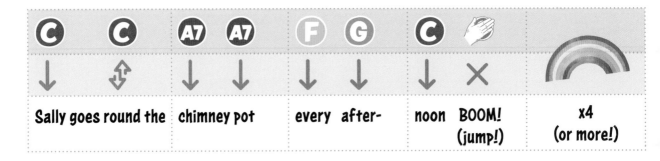

Practice & Shine Chart

Draw a checkmark, star, or any shape of your choice in the boxes.

FIRST TRY	THREE MORE TIMES	READY TO SHINE!
☐	☐ ☐ ☐	☐

Star Light, Star Bright

POPULAR NURSERY RHYME, ADAPTED FOR USE BY EMILY ARROW
CHORDS: C, Am, F, G

I love to look at the moon and the stars. Maybe you do too! This popular nursery rhyme is meant to be sung to the stars at night while you make a wish.

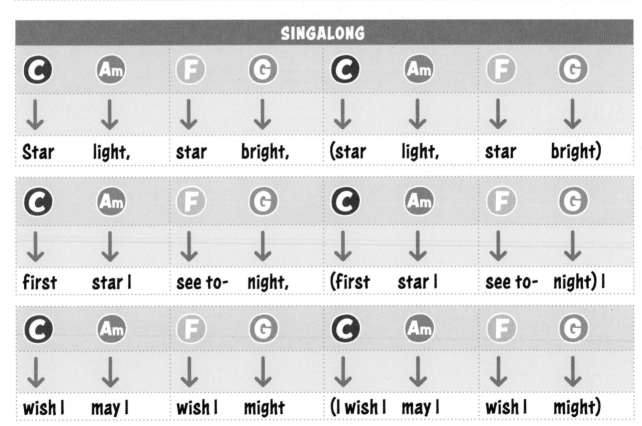

PATTERN PRACTICE

C   Am   F   G   C   Am   F   G   x2
↓   ↓   ↓   ↓   ↓   ↓   ↓   ↓

INTRODUCTION

C   Am   F   G   C   Am   F   G
↓   ↓   ↓   ↓   ↓   ↓   ↓   ↓

SINGALONG

C   Am   F   G   C   Am   F   G
↓   ↓   ↓   ↓   ↓   ↓   ↓   ↓
Star light, star bright, (star light, star bright)

C   Am   F   G   C   Am   F   G
↓   ↓   ↓   ↓   ↓   ↓   ↓   ↓
first star I see to-night, (first star I see to-night) I

C   Am   F   G   C   Am   F   G
↓   ↓   ↓   ↓   ↓   ↓   ↓   ↓
wish I may I wish I might (I wish I may I wish I might)

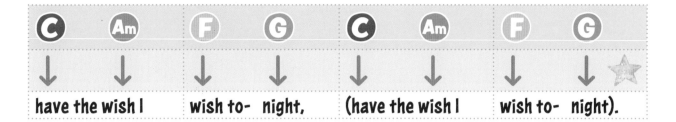

C	Am	F	G	C	Am	F	G
↓	↓	↓	↓	↓	↓	↓	↓ ⭐
have the wish I		wish to- night,		(have the wish I		wish to- night).	

PRACTICE & SHINE CHART

Draw a checkmark, star, or any shape of your choice in the boxes.

FIRST TRY	THREE MORE TIMES	READY TO SHINE!
☐	☐ ☐ ☐	☐

B-I-N-G-O

FOLK SONG
CHORDS: C, F, G, G7

Each new verse, we'll make new letters of the name Bingo disappear from the lyrics! Remember, when you see the , pat your ukulele instead of singing the letter.

SINGALONG

There . . . (sing before strumming)

C	C	F	C	C	G	C	C
↓↓	↓↓	↓↓	↓↓	↓↓	↓↓	↓	↓
was a	friend who	had a	dog and	Bingo	was her	name-	o!

C	C	F	F	G	G	C	C
↓	↓	↓↓	↓	↓	↓	↓↓	↓

1.	B	I	N-G	O,	B	I	N-G	O,
2.	🖐	I	N-G	O,	🖐	I	N-G	O,
3.	🖐	🖐	N-G	O,	🖐	🖐	N-G	O,
4.	🖐	🖐	🖐-G	O,	🖐	🖐	🖐-G	O,
5.	🖐	🖐	🖐-🖐	O,	🖐	🖐	🖐-🖐	O,
6.	🖐	🖐	🖐-🖐🖐,		🖐	🖐	🖐-🖐🖐,	

F	F	G	G	G7	G7	C	C
↓	↓	↓↓	↓↓	↓↓	↓↓	↓	↓
B	I	N-G	O and	Bin-go	was her	name-	o!
[clap]	I	N-G	O and	Bin-go	was her	name-	o!
[clap]	[clap]	N-G	O and	Bin-go	was her	name-	o!
[clap]	[clap]	[clap]-G	O and	Bin-go	was her	name-	o!
[clap]	[clap]	[clap]-[clap]	O and	Bin-go	was her	name-	o!
[clap]	[clap]	[clap]-[clap]	[clap] and	Bin-go	was her	name-	o! ⭐

(Rockstar Ending!)

PRACTICE & SHINE CHART

Draw a checkmark, star, or any shape of your choice in the boxes.

FIRST TRY

THREE MORE TIMES

READY TO SHINE!

The Alphabet Song (ABCs)

CHILDREN'S SONG
CHORDS: C, C7, F, G

To switch your left hand smoothly from **C** to **C7**, lift your **third finger** up after you play **C** and then use your **first finger** to play the **C7** chord.

PATTERN PRACTICE

C	C	C	C	C7	C7	C7	👏	🌈
↓	↓	↓	↓	↓	↓	↓	✕	x4

INTRODUCTION

F	F	C	C	G	G	C	👏
↓	↓	↓	↓	↓	↓	↓	✕

SINGALONG

C	C	C7	C7	F	F	C	👏
↓	↓	↓	↓	↓	↓	↓	✕
A	B	C	D	E	F	G	(pat!)

F	F	C	C	G	G	C	👏
↓	↓	↓	↓	⇕	⇕	↓	✕
H	I	J	K	L M	N O	P	(pat!)

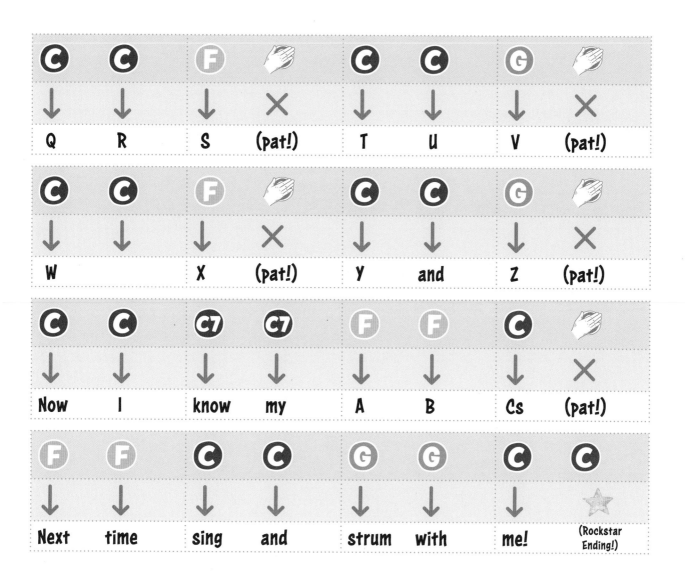

C	C	F	👏	C	C	G	👏
↓	↓	↓	×	↓	↓	↓	×
Q	R	S	(pat!)	T	U	V	(pat!)

C	C	F	👏	C	C	G	👏
↓	↓	↓	×	↓	↓	↓	×
W		X	(pat!)	Y	and	Z	(pat!)

C	C	C7	C7	F	F	C	👏
↓	↓	↓	↓	↓	↓	↓	×
Now	I	know	my	A	B	Cs	(pat!)

F	F	C	C	G	G	C	C
↓	↓	↓	↓	↓	↓	↓	⭐
Next	time	sing	and	strum	with	me!	(Rockstar Ending!)

PRACTICE & SHINE CHART

Draw a checkmark, star, or any shape of your choice in the boxes.

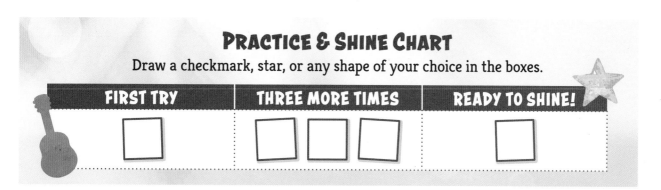

FIRST TRY	THREE MORE TIMES	READY TO SHINE!
☐	☐ ☐ ☐	☐

Head, Shoulders, Knees, and Toes

POPULAR CHILDREN'S SONG
CHORDS: C, G7, C7, F

You might know this popular song and its movements. It's so much fun to sing with others too, so you can strum while they do the movements.

PATTERN PRACTICE

C	C	C	C	C	C	C	C	
↓	↓	↕	↕	↓	↕	↓	↓	x4

SINGALONG

C	C	C	C	C	C	C	C
↓	↓	↕	↕	↓	↕	↓	↓
Head,		shoul-ders,	knees, and	toes,	knees and		toes

C	C	C	C	G7	G7	G7	G7
↓	↓	↕	↕	↓	↕	↓	↓
Head,		shoul-ders,	knees, and	toes,	knees and		toes

C		C7		F	F	F	F
↓		↓		↕	↕	↓	↓
Eyes and		ears and		mouth	and		nose

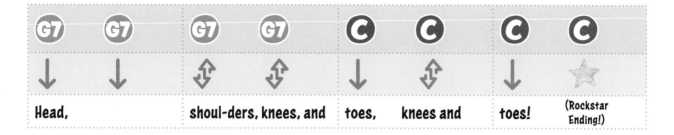

G7	G7	G7	G7	C	C	C	C
↓	↓	⇕	⇕	↓	⇕	↓	⭐
Head,		shoul-ders, knees, and		toes,	knees and	toes!	(Rockstar Ending!)

PRACTICE & SHINE CHART

Draw a checkmark, star, or any shape of your choice in the boxes.

FIRST TRY	THREE MORE TIMES	READY TO SHINE!
☐	☐ ☐ ☐	☐

head

shoulders

knees

and toes!

The Wheels on the Bus

POPULAR CHILDREN'S SONG

CHORDS: C, G

This song has more than one **verse**. Each time you sing the song, you'll sing the lyrics of a new verse until you've sung all four verses. Each verse is color-coded to help you stay on track.

SINGALONG

The . . . (sing before strumming)

C ↓	C ↓↓	C ↓	C ↓	C ↓	C ↓	C ↓	👋 ✗
1. wheels	**on the**	**bus**	**go**	**round**	**and**	**round,**	**(pat!)**
2. wipers	on the	bus	go	swish	swish	swish,	(pat!)
3. people	on the	bus	go	up	and	down,	(pat!)
4. horn	on the	bus	goes	beep	beep	beep,	(pat!)

G ↓	G ↓	G ↓	👋 ✗	C ↓	C ↓	C ↓	C ↓
round	**and**	**round,**	**(pat!)**	**round**	**and**	**round,**	**the**
swish	swish	swish,	(pat!)	swish	swish	swish,	the
up	and	down,	(pat!)	up	and	down,	the
beep	beep	beep,	(pat!)	beep	beep	beep,	the

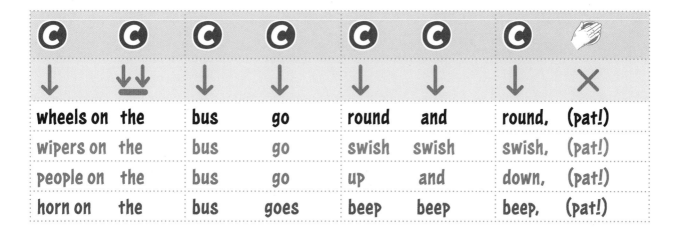

C	C	C	C	C	C	C	👏
↓	↓↓	↓	↓	↓	↓	↓	✗
wheels on	the	bus	go	round	and	round,	(pat!)
wipers on	the	bus	go	swish	swish	swish,	(pat!)
people on	the	bus	go	up	and	down,	(pat!)
horn on	the	bus	goes	beep	beep	beep,	(pat!)

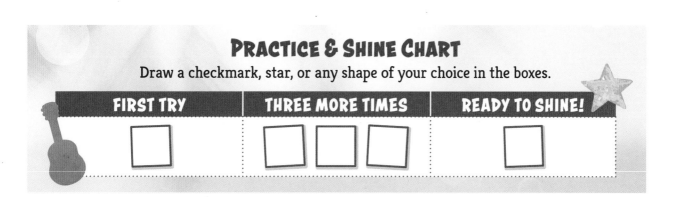

G	G	G	G	C	C	C	👏
↓	↓	↓	↓	↓	↓	↓	✗
all		through	the	town!			The . . .
all		through	the	town!			The . . .
all		through	the	town!			The . . .
all		through	the	town!			⭐ (Rockstar Ending!)

PRACTICE & SHINE CHART

Draw a checkmark, star, or any shape of your choice in the boxes.

FIRST TRY	THREE MORE TIMES	READY TO SHINE!
☐	☐ ☐ ☐	☐

Happy Birthday to You

POPULAR FOLK SONG
CHORDS: C, G7, F, G

Do you recognize this song from birthday celebrations? Now you can bring your ukulele and strum along!

SINGALONG

Happy . . . (sing before strumming)

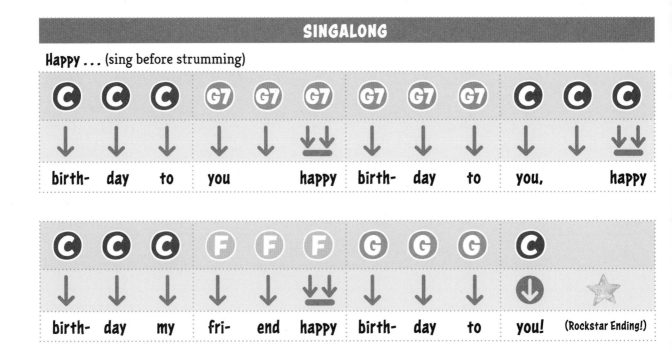

PRACTICE & SHINE CHART

Draw a checkmark, star, or any shape of your choice in the boxes.

Fingerpicking Song

BY EMILY ARROW
CHORDS: 0 = OPEN STRINGS

Fingerpicking is when you pick each string on its own instead of strumming your fingers along the strings. For the fingerpicking songs in this book, each finger gets its own string!

G string (4, top string)	C string (3)	E string (2)	A string (1)
THUMB	FIRST FINGER	SECOND FINGER	THIRD FINGER

In this song, your left hand will play **open strings**, or 0 chord shapes, while the fingers of your right hand pluck G, C, E, A one string at a time, just like when you're tuning.

SINGALONG

LEFT HAND: 0 = Open strings | **RIGHT HAND:** fingerpicking the strings

G C E A	G C E A	G C E A	G C E A
G C E A	from the top string	G C E A	fin- ger- pick- ing

G C E A	G C E A	G C E A	G C E A
G C E A	thumb, one, two, three	G C E A	fin- ger- pick- ing!

PRACTICE & SHINE CHART

Draw a checkmark, star, or any shape of your choice in the boxes.

FIRST TRY	THREE MORE TIMES	READY TO SHINE!
☐	☐ ☐ ☐	☐

The Music in Me

BY EMILY ARROW

CHORDS: 0 = OPEN STRINGS

This very special song began as a poem. It can be sung many times in a row to celebrate the music in all of us.

To play, your left hand will play open strings and your right hand will fingerpick the strings in the pattern G, C, E, A. To sing along, follow and match the string's musical pitches with your voice.

SINGALONG

LEFT HAND: 0 = Open strings

RIGHT HAND:

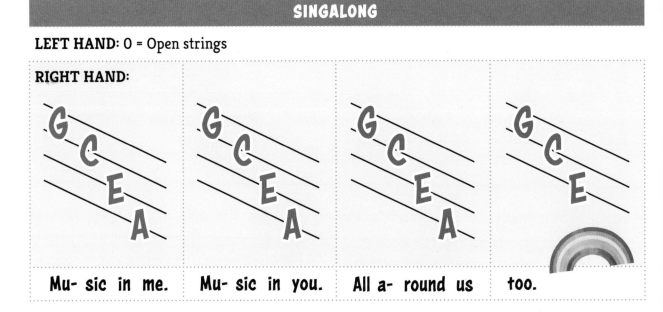

Mu- sic in me.	Mu- sic in you.	All a- round us	too.

PRACTICE & SHINE CHART

Draw a checkmark, star, or any shape of your choice in the boxes.

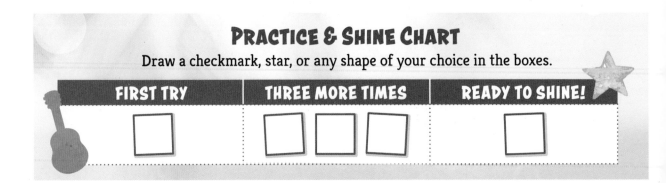

FIRST TRY	THREE MORE TIMES	READY TO SHINE!
☐	☐ ☐ ☐	☐

Rain, Rain, Go Away

CHILDREN'S SONG, LYRICS ADAPTED FOR USE BY EMILY ARROW
CHORDS: C, G

Versions of this popular song have origins in many parts of the world, including Ghana, Africa, and as a nursery rhyme in England. As you sing and play this song on your ukulele, can you imagine the fingerpicking pattern is the gentle sound of raindrops falling from the sky?

In this song, your left hand will press down to make chord shapes. Notice how the G, C, E, A fingerpicking pattern in your right hand repeats twice during each phrase.

SINGALONG

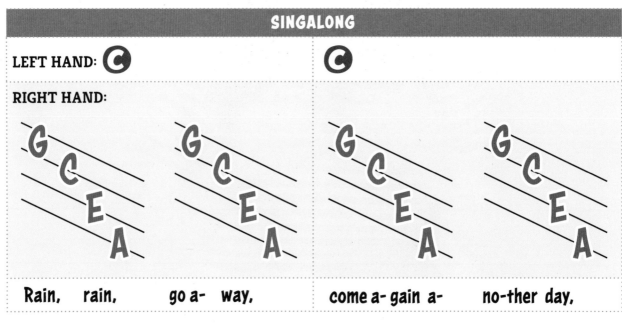

LEFT HAND: C   C

RIGHT HAND:

Rain,   rain,   go a- way,   come a- gain a-   no-ther day,

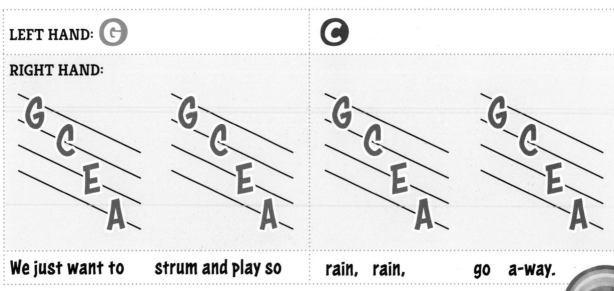

LEFT HAND: G   C

RIGHT HAND:

We just want to   strum and play so   rain, rain,   go   a-way.

58

PRACTICE & SHINE CHART

Draw a checkmark, star, or any shape of your choice in the boxes.

FIRST TRY	THREE MORE TIMES	READY TO SHINE!
☐	☐ ☐ ☐	☐

The More We Get Together

POPULAR CHILDREN'S SONG
CHORDS: C, G, G7

The song "The More We Get Together" is sung by young people around the world. Here are some examples of the song's title in multiple languages:

- **"The More We Get Together"** in the United States (English)
- **"Bila kita berkumpul"** in Singapore (Malay)
- **"Cuanto más juntos estemos"** (Spanish)
- **"Plus nous serons ensemble"** (French)

We'll learn the version commonly sung in the United States.

PATTERN PRACTICE

Did you notice there are three down strum arrows in each box instead of two like usual? Pay attention to how this different groove feels while you play!

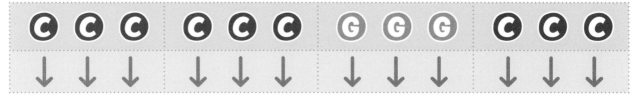

SINGALONG

Oh the . . . (sing before strumming)

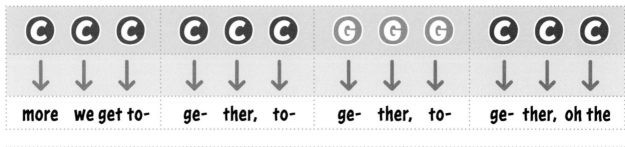

more we get to- ge- ther, to- ge- ther, to- ge- ther, oh the

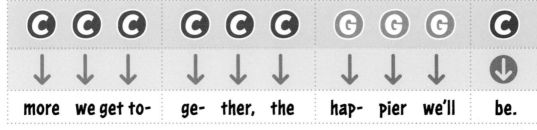

more we get to- ge- ther, the hap- pier we'll be.

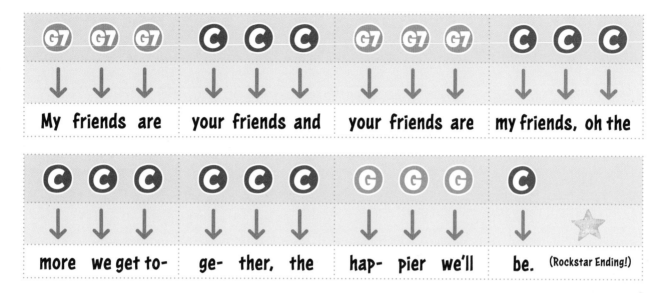

G7 G7 G7	C C C	G7 G7 G7	C C C
↓ ↓ ↓	↓ ↓ ↓	↓ ↓ ↓	↓ ↓ ↓
My friends are	your friends and	your friends are	my friends, oh the

C C C	C C C	G G G	C
↓ ↓ ↓	↓ ↓ ↓	↓ ↓ ↓	↓ ⭐
more we get to-	ge- ther, the	hap- pier we'll	be. (Rockstar Ending!)

PRACTICE & SHINE CHART

Draw a checkmark, star, or any shape of your choice in the boxes.

FIRST TRY

☐

THREE MORE TIMES

☐ ☐ ☐

READY TO SHINE!

☐

If You're Happy and You Know It

POPULAR CHILDREN'S SONG, LYRICS ADAPTED FOR USE BY EMILY ARROW

CHORDS: C, G, F

This is one of my favorite songs to sing and strum! Notice most lines end in the ⬇ whole strum. That means you'll strum the chord, then wait for the following beat to pass before strumming the next chord.

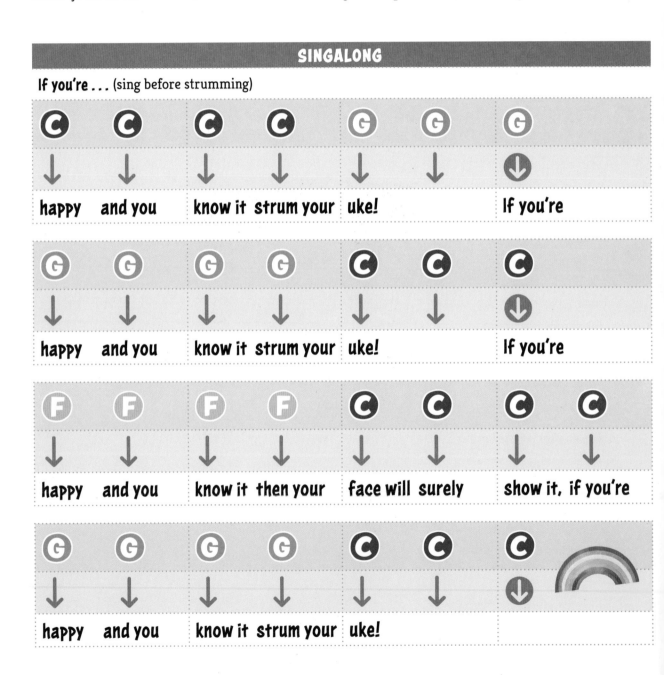

SINGALONG

If you're . . . (sing before strumming)

PRACTICE & SHINE CHART

Draw a checkmark, star, or any shape of your choice in the boxes.

FIRST TRY	THREE MORE TIMES	READY TO SHINE!
☐	☐ ☐ ☐	☐

A Ram Sam Sam

POPULAR MOROCCAN CHILDREN'S SONG

CHORDS: C, G, C7, F

The song "A Ram Sam Sam" is a popular song for children in Morocco. Morocco is on the northwest coast of Africa and this song is sung in Arabic. The lyrics "a ram sam sam" don't have a meaning. The lyrics "guli" and "a rafiq" translate to mean telling something to a friend, specifically a friend you travel with. Practice pronouncing the lyrics and then strum and sing along!

a ram sam sam (no meaning)

guli guli sounds like *goo-lee goo-lee* (tell me tell me)

a rafiq sounds like *uh raa-fee*—the "q" is silent (a friend)

After you strum and sing, try putting your ukulele down and doing the movements while you sing the lyrics aloud (see facing page).

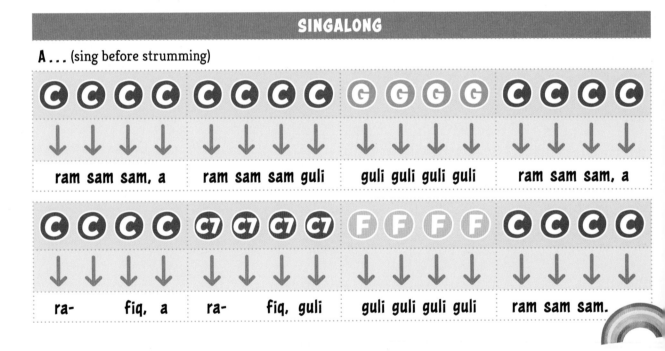

SINGALONG

A . . . (sing before strumming)

| C C C C | C C C C | G G G G | C C C C |
| ram sam sam, a | ram sam sam guli | guli guli guli guli | ram sam sam, a |

| C C C C | C7 C7 C7 C7 | F F F F | C C C C |
| ra-   fiq, a | ra-   fiq, guli | guli guli guli guli | ram sam sam. |

PRACTICE & SHINE CHART

Draw a checkmark, star, or any shape of your choice in the boxes.

FIRST TRY	THREE MORE TIMES	READY TO SHINE!
☐	☐ ☐ ☐	☐

During the lyrics
a ram sam sam:
pat your legs to the beat

During the lyrics
guli guli:
roll fists over each other in a circle

During the lyrics
a rafiq:
spread arms wide apart . . .

. . . and then back!

You can sing in your own style
or listen to the recording at
www.emilyarrow.com/ukulelesongs
to sing along.

Making A Pizza Bop! Bop!

BY EMILY ARROW

CHORDS: G7, A7, C7, C

Let's imagine you're making a pizza and choosing which toppings to add. The question part of the song will ask what you're going to put on top of the pizza, and the response section is where you'll choose something you'd like to add on top. Sing and strum along!

QUESTION

G7	G7	A7	A7	G7	G7	C	C
↓	↓	↓	↓	↓	↓	↓	↓
Making a	pizza	bop	bop!	Whatcha	gonna put on	top	top?

RESPONSES

I'll put . . . (sing before strumming)

C7	C7	A7	A7	C7	C7	G7	👏
↓	↓	↓	↓	↓	↓	↓	✕
Cheese,	cheese on	top	top,	cheese,	cheese on	top	STOP!

C7	C7	A7	A7	C7	C7	G7	👏
↓	↓	↓	↓	↓	↓	↓	✕
Red to-	matoes on	top	top,	red to-	matoes on	top	STOP!

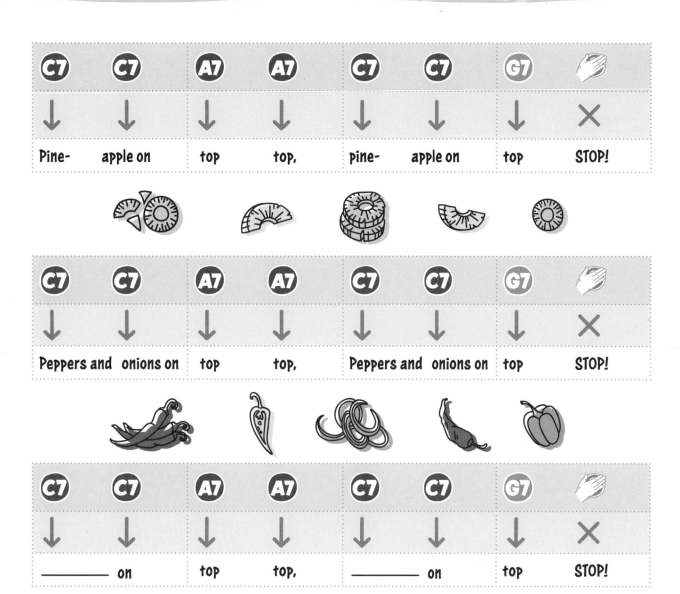

C7	C7	A7	A7	C7	C7	G7	👏
↓	↓	↓	↓	↓	↓	↓	✕
Pine-	apple on	top	top,	pine-	apple on	top	STOP!

C7	C7	A7	A7	C7	C7	G7	👏
↓	↓	↓	↓	↓	↓	↓	✕
Peppers and onions on		top	top,	Peppers and onions on		top	STOP!

C7	C7	A7	A7	C7	C7	G7	👏
↓	↓	↓	↓	↓	↓	↓	✕
_____ on		top	top,	_____ on		top	STOP!

PRACTICE & SHINE CHART

Draw a checkmark, star, or any shape of your choice in the boxes.

FIRST TRY	THREE MORE TIMES	READY TO SHINE!
☐	☐ ☐ ☐	☐

Two Little Apples

AMERICAN FOLK RHYME

CHORDS: C, G, F

Let's turn one of my favorite rhymes into a song by adding chords to the lyrics. Begin by saying the rhyme aloud with hand movements! Then strum and sing along to the lyrics in your own way.

Lyrics
1. Two little apples hanging in a tree,
2. Two little apples smiled at me,
3. I shook that tree as hard as I could, and
4. down came the apples!
5. Mmm, they were good.

Hand Movements
1. Put your hands in the air above your head.
2. Make fists with your hands like two apples.
3. Pretend to shake the tree.
4. Wiggle your fingers down like falling apples.
5. Rub your belly. Mmm!

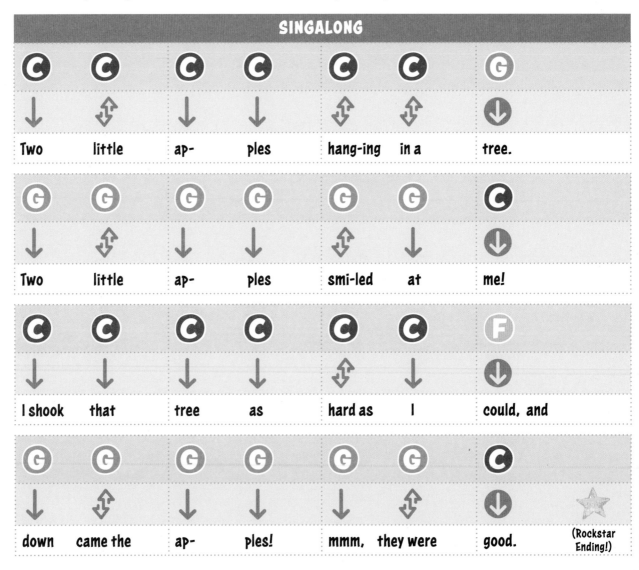

PRACTICE & SHINE CHART

Draw a checkmark, star, or any shape of your choice in the boxes.

FIRST TRY	THREE MORE TIMES	READY TO SHINE!
☐	☐ ☐ ☐	☐

Books! Books!

BY EMILY ARROW AND GRACE KELLY

CHORDS: C, F, G

Learn how I sing the song (and sing along!) by visiting
www.emilyarrow.com/ukulelesongs

This is a song I wrote because I love books sooooo much. You can sing like I do (visit *www.emilyarrow.com/ukulelesongs*), or you can create your own way of singing along to the chords. Grab your favorite book and get ready to sing!

SINGALONG - VERSE

C	C	F	C	F	F	G	G
↓	↓	↓	↓	↓	↓	↓	↓
Look around,	look around,	what do	you see?	Books!	Books! Are you	ready to	read?

C	C	F	C	F	F	G	C
↓	↓	↓	↓	↓	↓	↓	⬇
Gather 'round,	gather 'round,	what do you hear?		Books!	Books! Open	up your	ears,

SINGALONG - CHORUS

I'll read to . . . (sing before strumming)

F	F	F	F	C	C	C	C
↓	↓	↓	↓	↓	↓	↓	↓
you	you	you,	you'll sing to	me	me	me.	

G	G	G	G	F	F	C	C
↓	↓	↓	↓	↓	↓	↓	↓
Bo-	oks!	Bo-	oks!	Everybody	find a	seat!	I'll read to

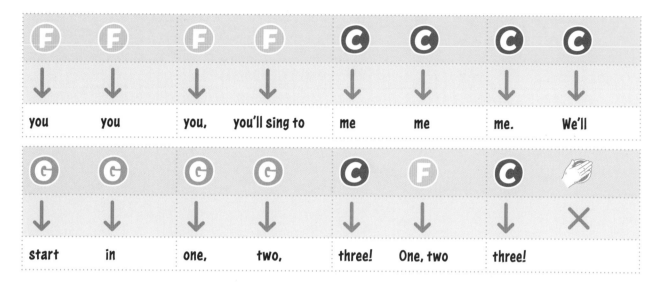

F	F	F	F	C	C	C	C
↓	↓	↓	↓	↓	↓	↓	↓
you	you	you,	you'll sing to	me	me	me.	We'll

G	G	G	G	C	F	C	
↓	↓	↓	↓	↓	↓	↓	✕
start	in	one,	two,	three!	One, two	three!	

PRACTICE & SHINE CHART

Draw a checkmark, star, or any shape of your choice in the boxes.

FIRST TRY

☐

THREE MORE TIMES

☐ ☐ ☐

READY TO SHINE!

☐

Down By the Bay

POPULAR FOLK SONG

CHORDS: C, G

This song begins with the **chorus**, and then we sing many different (and silly!) **verses**. You can even try writing your own lyrics in the Verse section.

PATTERN PRACTICE

Try the **down-down** (wait) **up-down** pattern below before singing and playing it together.

SINGALONG - CHORUS

Down by the . . . (sing before strumming)

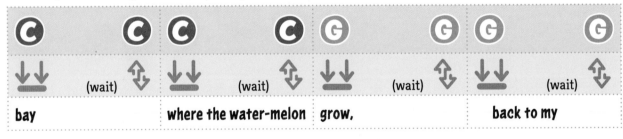

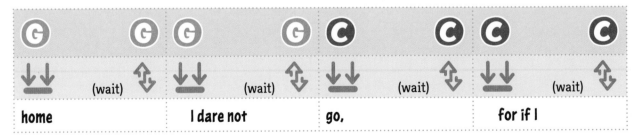

F		F	F		F	C		C	C
↓↓ (wait)		⇕	↓↓	(wait)	⇕	↓↓ (wait)		⇕	↓
do			my friends would			say:			Have you . . .

SINGALONG - VERSE

C	👏	C	👏	G		G	C	
↓ (wait)	✕	↓ (wait)	✕	↓↓ (wait)		⇕	⬇	

#				
1.	ever seen a bear	combing their hair?	Down by the	bay!
2.	ever seen a fly	wearing a tie?	Down by the	bay!
3.	ever seen a whale	with a polka-dot tail?	Down by the	bay!
4.	ever seen a llama	wearing pajamas?	Down by the	bay!
5.	ever seen a _____	_____?	Down by the	bay!

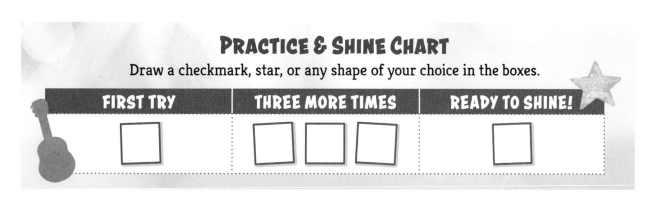

PRACTICE & SHINE CHART

Draw a checkmark, star, or any shape of your choice in the boxes.

FIRST TRY	THREE MORE TIMES	READY TO SHINE!
☐	☐ ☐ ☐	☐

If All the Raindrops

FOLK SONG, LYRICS ADAPTED FOR USE BY EMILY ARROW

CHORDS: C, Am, Dm, G, F

Can you imagine if raindrops were music notes and lollipops? Or snowflakes and milkshakes? Or sunbeams and ice cream? Use your imagination to sing along to this silly song!

SINGALONG - VERSE							

If . . . (sing before strumming)

C ↓	C ↕	Am ↓	Am ↕	Dm ↓	Dm ↕	G ↓	G ↕
1. all	the	rain-	drops were	music	notes and	lolli-	pops,
2. all	the	snow-	flakes were	music	notes and	milk-	shakes,
3. all	the	sun-	beams were	music	notes and	ice	cream,
4. all	the	rain-	drops were	music	notes and	lolli-	pops,

C ↓	C ↕	G ↓	G ↕	C ↓	G ↓	C ↓	✋ ✕ ⬢
oh	what a	rain	that would	be.			(After the 4th verse, stop here!)

SINGALONG - CHORUS							

C ↓	C ↕	F ↓	F ↕	C ↓	C ↕	G ↓	✋ ✕
Stand-	ing out-	side	with your	mouth	op-en	wide,	

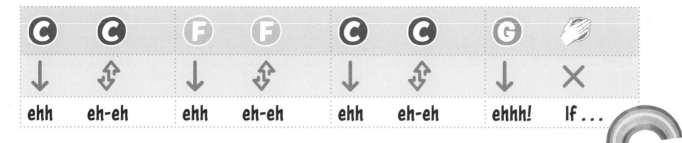

C	C	F	F	C	C	G	👏
↓	↕	↓	↕	↓	↕	↓	✕
ehh	eh-eh	ehh	eh-eh	ehh	eh-eh	ehhh!	If . . .

PRACTICE & SHINE CHART

Draw a checkmark, star, or any shape of your choice in the boxes.

FIRST TRY

THREE MORE TIMES

READY TO SHINE!

The Bear Went Over the Mountain

FOLK SONG

CHORDS: F, G7, C, G

Do you love to spend time in nature? I love to hike and be outdoors. This is a fun song about a bear on a big adventure in the mountains, forest, trees, and river. This is a perfect song to strum and sing while you're on an adventure yourself—whether you're hiking up a mountain or exploring at the park!

INTRODUCTION

F	F	G7	G7	C	C	C	C	
↓	↓	↓	↓	↓	↓	↓	↓	🌈 x2

SINGALONG

The . . . (sing before strumming)

C	C	F	C	G	G	C	C
↓	↓	↓	↓	↓	↓	↓	↓

1.	bear went	over the	moun-	tain, the	bear went	over the	moun-	tain, the
2.	bear went	into the	for-	est, the	bear went	into the	for-	est, the
3.	bear climbed up in the		tall	trees, the	bear climbed up in the		tall	trees, the
4.	bear went	through the	ri-	ver, the	bear went	through the	ri-	ver, the

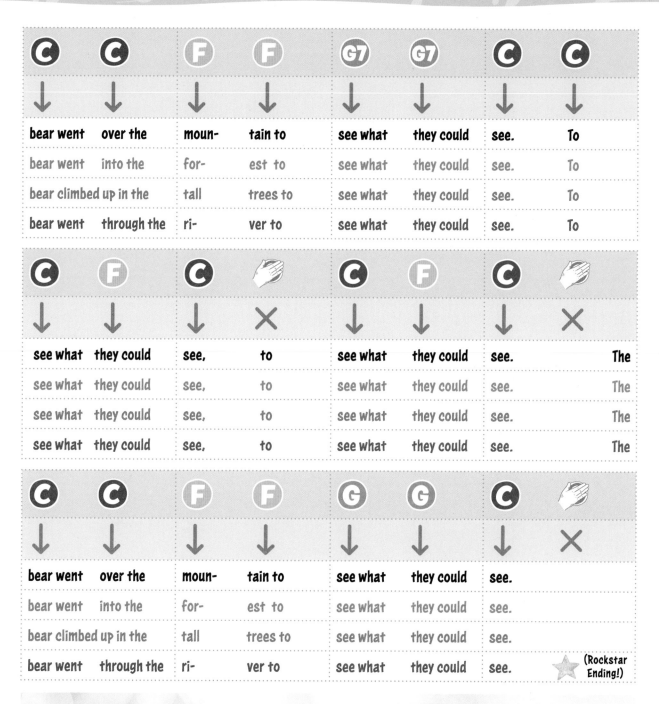

PRACTICE & SHINE CHART

Draw a checkmark, star, or any shape of your choice in the boxes.

FIRST TRY	THREE MORE TIMES			READY TO SHINE!
☐	☐	☐	☐	☐

LEARN: How to Play Melody on the Ukulele

The **melody** is the tune of a song. On ukulele, we play the melody by playing *one string at a time* instead of strumming all of the strings together.

These numbers are the fret numbers:

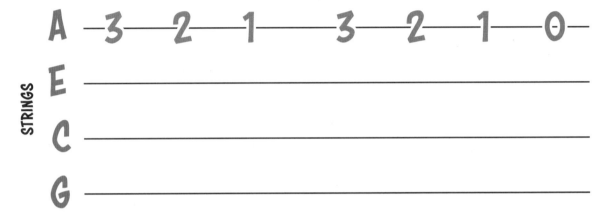

STRINGS

A — 3 — 2 — 1 — 3 — 2 — 1 — 0 —
E
C
G

In this melody, the 3 at the beginning of the song means you would push down on the 3rd fret of the **A** string (bottom string). Continuing next to the 2nd fret, then 1st fret on the A string.

When you see 0, that means **open strings**, so your left hand won't push down on any frets.

Count the Frets Song

BY EMILY ARROW

Play this song melody by plucking each string with your <u>right thumb</u>.

Remember, when you see 0, that means to play the string **open**. When you see 1, 2, or 3, it means to push down on the string right above that fret number's line.

MELODY SINGALONG

STRINGS

A — 3 — 2 — 1 — 3 — 2 — 1 —
E —————————————————————————
C —————————————————————————
G —————————————————————————

Three,   two,   one,   count   the   frets.

STRINGS

A —————————————————————————
E — 1 — 2 — 3 — 1 — 2 — 3 —
C —————————————————————————
G —————————————————————————

One,   two,   three,   E   string   next!

STRINGS

A —————————————————————————
E —————————————————————————
C — 3 — 2 — 1 — 3 — 2 — 1 —
G —————————————————————————

Three,   two,   one,   count   the   frets.

STRINGS

A —————————————————————————
E —————————————————————————
C — 1 — 2 — 3 — 1 — 2 — 3 —
G —————————————————————————

One,   two,   three,   C   string   next!

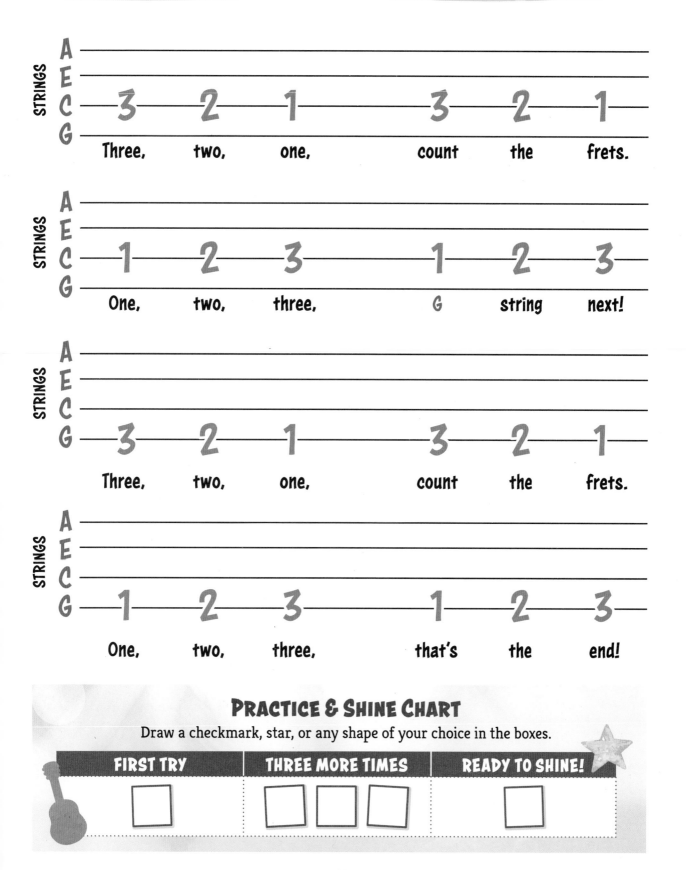

STRINGS

A
E
3 **2** **1** **3** **2** **1**
C
G

Three,   two,   one,   count   the   frets.

STRINGS

A
E
1 **2** **3** **1** **2** **3**
C
G

One,   two,   three,   G   string   next!

STRINGS

A
E
C
3 **2** **1** **3** **2** **1**
G

Three,   two,   one,   count   the   frets.

STRINGS

A
E
C
1 **2** **3** **1** **2** **3**
G

One,   two,   three,   that's   the   end!

PRACTICE & SHINE CHART

Draw a checkmark, star, or any shape of your choice in the boxes.

FIRST TRY	THREE MORE TIMES	READY TO SHINE!
☐	☐ ☐ ☐	☐

Bow Wow Wow

FOLK SONG

Play this song melody by plucking each string with your <u>right thumb</u>.

When you see 0, that means to play the string **open**. This entire song is played on the open string, or 0, so you won't need to press down on any frets with your left hand.

Motions: Standing up, stomp your feet three times on the lyrics, "bow wow wow!"

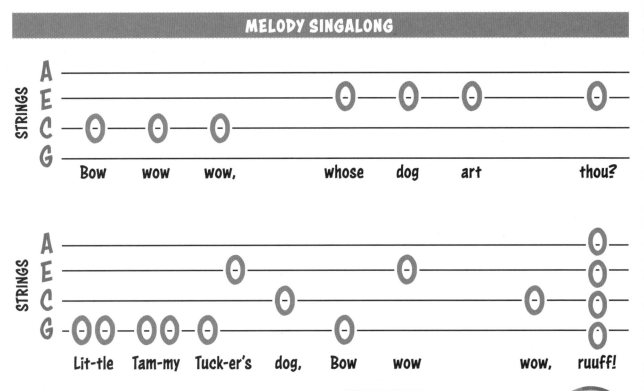

MELODY SINGALONG

STRINGS A E C G

Bow   wow   wow,   whose   dog   art   thou?

STRINGS A E C G

Lit-tle   Tam-my   Tuck-er's   dog,   Bow   wow   wow,   ruuff!

When you see numbers on all of the strings, play a strum!

PRACTICE & SHINE CHART

Draw a checkmark, star, or any shape of your choice in the boxes.

FIRST TRY	THREE MORE TIMES	READY TO SHINE!
☐	☐ ☐ ☐	☐

Twinkle, Twinkle, Little Star

POPULAR NURSERY RHYME

Before playing the melody of "Twinkle, Twinkle, Little Star," read the song with your eyes. Then respond to a few questions:

1. Which two strings are used in this song? _____ string and _____ string

2. There are two sections in the song, labeled as ♥ and ⭐ . Circle which of the shapes is played twice: ♥ ⭐

3. Which fret number does the song begin *and* end on? _____ Hint: this number means to play open strings.

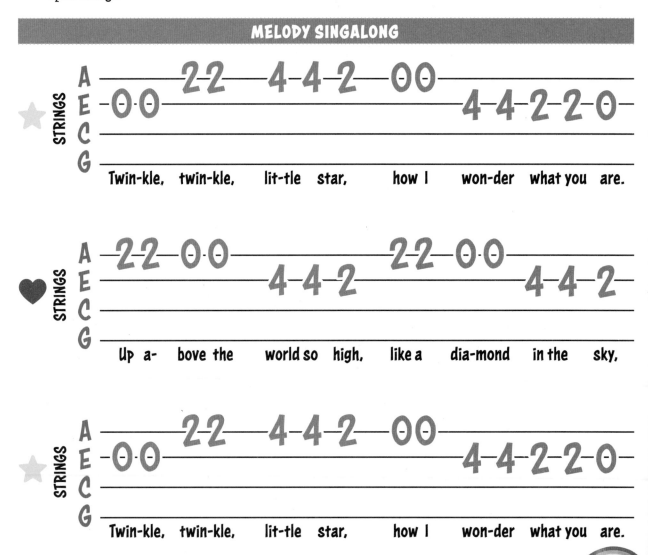

MELODY SINGALONG

STRINGS A / E / C / G

Twin-kle, twin-kle, lit-tle star, how I won-der what you are.

Up a- bove the world so high, like a dia-mond in the sky,

Twin-kle, twin-kle, lit-tle star, how I won-der what you are.

PRACTICE & SHINE CHART

Draw a checkmark, star, or any shape of your choice in the boxes.

FIRST TRY	THREE MORE TIMES	READY TO SHINE!
☐	☐ ☐ ☐	☐

London Bridge

TRADITIONAL SONG

Before playing the melody of "London Bridge," read the song first with your eyes. Then respond to a few questions:

1. Which three strings are used in this song? _____ string, _____ string, and _____ string

2. Which fret number does the song end on? _____ Hint: this number means to play open strings.

MELODY SINGALONG

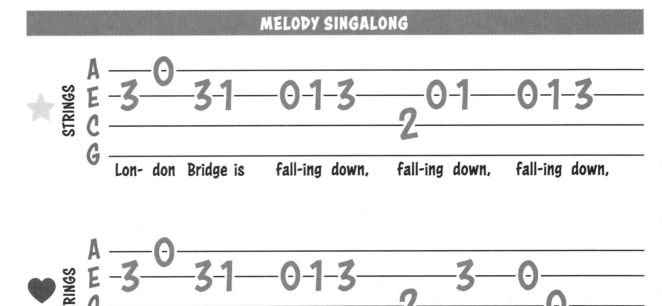

PRACTICE & SHINE CHART

Draw a checkmark, star, or any shape of your choice in the boxes.

Write Your Own Songs

Are you ready to let your creativity run wild? In this section you'll find:

- A fast and easy method for writing your own songs

- A song template to sing about a place you love

- A song template to sing about an awesome friend

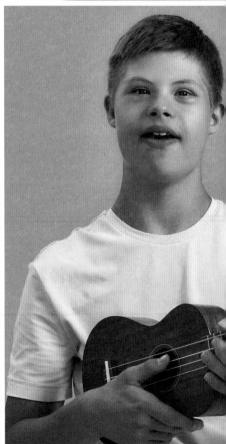

- Blank song templates for you to write your own unique songs!

LISTEN FIRST!
To listen and strum
along to these
songs, visit
www.emilyarrow.com/
ukulelesongs

LEARN: How to Write Your Own Songs

Writing a song is kind of like creating a watercolor painting. To create a watercolor painting, you'd need watercolor paints.

In songwriting, let's imagine the paints are the color dot chords—they're even colorful like paints! To write a song, you'll choose which chords to use and when to play them.

And just like combining paints with water, when you strum and sing on your ukulele, you're creating your very own masterpiece! Imagine that instead of using your paintbrush to create shapes and lines, you're using your voice as a paintbrush to create music and **lyrics**, or the words you sing in a song.

CHORDS FOR SONGWRITING

THE RHYME-ANGLE TRIANGLE

When you're writing lyrics and you see the **rhyme-angle triangle** , it gives you the idea to make the words rhyme with each other. Here's an example:

I love <u>dogs</u>   I love <u>frogs</u>

In this book, the songwriting pages have helpful clues to guide you!

To write your own songs:

- add chords in the blank circles ◯
- write your own lyrics on the blank lines _____
- write rhyming words when you see the rhyme-angle triangle ▲

HERE'S AN EXAMPLE:

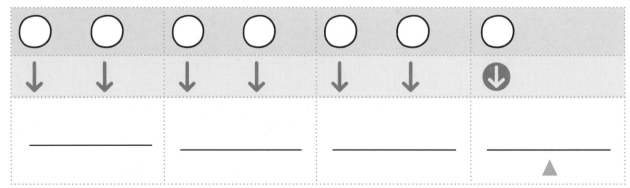

Songwriting:
A Place I Love Song

Think of a place you love to go to or visit. Some ideas could be the park, the library, a friend's house, the forest, a place you've traveled to, the place you live, or your classroom at school.

In the box, write or draw about a place you love.

To get started with this song, write the name of the place on the line below to give your song a title! Your title might be more than one single word, for example: "The Music Studio Song."

The _____ Song
(a place I love)

I   love   _____ ,   it's   so   _____ ,

(the place that you love)   (a word to describe it)

when   I'm   there,   I   feel   _____ .

(a feeling)

Oh I   love   _____ ,   it's   so   great,

(the place you love)

Let's   go   there   right   now,   to-   day!

Songwriting: Song for a Friend

Think of a friend or a special person in your life who you'd like to write a song about.

In this box, draw a picture of the friend your song will be about.

In this box, write words that describe your friend.

For example, you could write the words "funny" or "kind."

It will be so special when you write and then share the song with them!

My Friend _____
(your friend's name)

My   friend   _____,   you   are   _____,
(your friend's name)   (word that describes them)

my   friend   _____,   you   are   _____,
(your friend's name)   (word that describes them)

I'm   so   grate-   ful   we   are   friends,

now   I'll   sing   it   all   a-   gain!

Blank Song Templates

Here is where you can let your creativity completely loose! After all this playing and learning, you must be excited to write your own songs from scratch. Let's get started!

Fill in the circles with your chosen chords

Fill in the bottom row with your lyrics
(rhyme when you see the rhyme-angle triangle ▲ !)

Fill in the middle row with your choice of strumming arrows!

Practice tracing the different types of strumming arrows here:

EXAMPLE

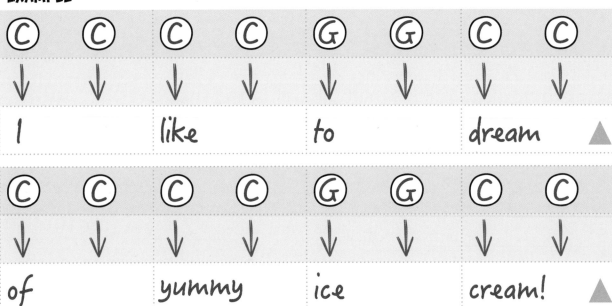

Song Title: _____

By: _____ Date: _____

LINE 1

◯ ◯ ◯ ◯ ◯ ◯ ◯ ◯

LINE 2

◯ ◯ ◯ ◯ ◯ ◯ ◯ ◯

LINE 3

◯ ◯ ◯ ◯ ◯ ◯ ◯ ◯

LINE 4

◯ ◯ ◯ ◯ ◯ ◯ ◯ ◯

Song Title: _____

By: _____ Date: _____

LINE 1

◯　◯　◯　◯　◯　◯　◯　◯

LINE 2

◯　◯　◯　◯　◯　◯　◯　◯

LINE 3

◯　◯　◯　◯　◯　◯　◯　◯

LINE 4

◯　◯　◯　◯　◯　◯　◯　◯

Song Title: _____

By: _____ Date: _____

LINE 1

○ ○ ○ ○ ○ ○ ○ ○

LINE 2

○ ○ ○ ○ ○ ○ ○ ○

LINE 3

○ ○ ○ ○ ○ ○ ○ ○

LINE 4

○ ○ ○ ○ ○ ○ ○ ○

Song Title: _____

By: _____ Date: _____

LINE 1

LINE 2

LINE 3

LINE 4

Song Title: _____

By: _____ **Date:** _____

LINE 1

LINE 2

LINE 3

LINE 4

Song Title: _____

By: _____ Date: _____

LINE 1

LINE 2

LINE 3

LINE 4

Song Title: _____

By: _____ Date: _____

LINE 1

LINE 2

LINE 3

LINE 4

Song Title: _____

By: _____ Date: _____

LINE 1

○ ○   ○ ○   ○ ○   ○ ○

LINE 2

○ ○   ○ ○   ○ ○   ○ ○

▲

LINE 3

○ ○   ○ ○   ○ ○   ○ ○

LINE 4

○ ○   ○ ○   ○ ○   ○ ○

▲

Song Title: _____

By: _____ Date: _____

LINE 1

LINE 2

LINE 3

LINE 4

Practice Journey

Try practicing about 4 times a week for 10 minutes (or so)!

Each time you practice, fill in the box with your own "sticker" by drawing something fun. Decide how you'll celebrate when you reach the ukulele at the end! Then you get to start the journey all over again.

START

WEEK: _____

WEEK: _____

WEEK: _____

WEEK: _____

WEEK: _____

How I plan to celebrate reaching the end of my Practice Journey:

END

_____

START

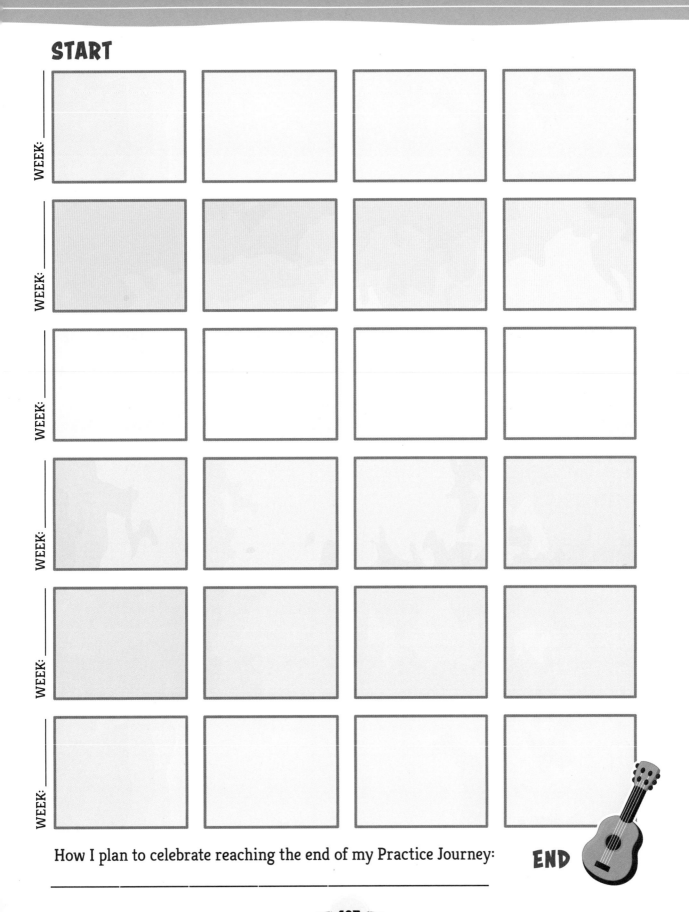

WEEK: ___

WEEK: ___

WEEK: ___

WEEK: ___

WEEK: ___

WEEK: ___

How I plan to celebrate reaching the end of my Practice Journey:

_____

END

START

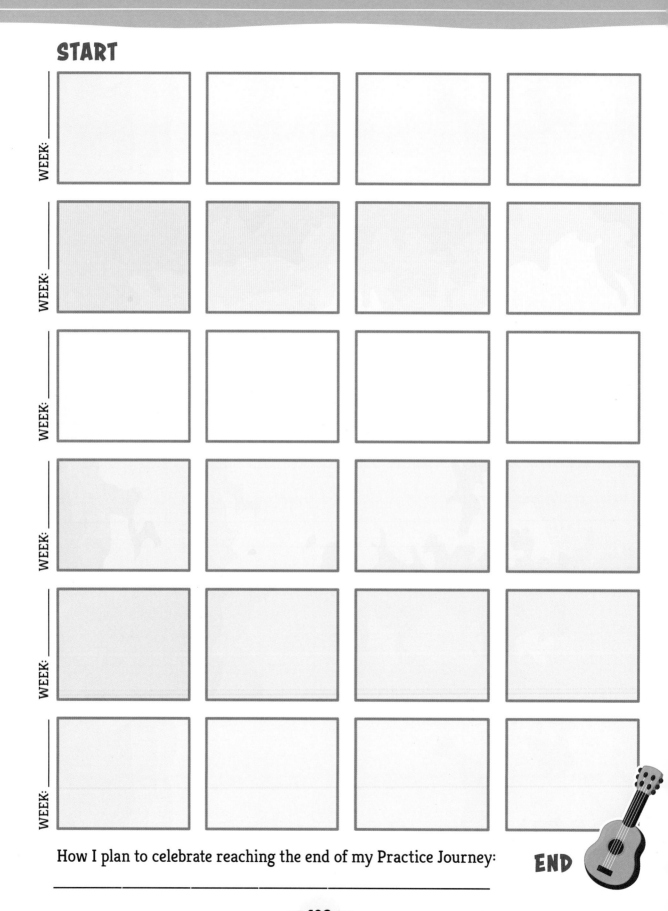

WEEK:

WEEK:

WEEK:

WEEK:

WEEK:

WEEK:

How I plan to celebrate reaching the end of my Practice Journey:

END

START

WEEK: _____

WEEK: _____

WEEK: _____

WEEK: _____

WEEK: _____

WEEK: _____

How I plan to celebrate reaching the end of my Practice Journey:

END

Index

About the Author

Emily Arrow is an award-winning childrens' songwriter on a mission to inspire a young generation through the joy of music. A popular YouTube personality, Emily's kindie music albums are now a family music sensation with #1 songs on *SiriusXM's Kids' Place Live*! Emily began her career as a K-6 music teacher after earning her music degree at Berklee College of Music. She is the author of multiple books for young people, including *Kids' Guide to Learning the Ukulele* (Happy Fox Books).

Emily and her ukulele, Bow, tour bookstores and venues around the country to help young people navigate big feelings **the "Arrow" way**: through art, with heart. When she's not on the road, Emily splits her time between Nashville, Los Angeles, and Portland, Oregon. And she loves to go on walks with her rockstar rescue dog named Laika (who makes a few appearances in this book!).

Find more resources and play along to the songs by visiting *www.EmilyArrow.com*.

Praise for This Book

"This fun-filled book is jam-packed with advice, inspiration, and activities to get beginning music-makers and aspiring singer-songwriters up and running."

—Gareth Dylan Smith, Assistant Professor of Music, Music Education, Boston University

"This is so much more than a songbook—it's interactive, engaging, and even provides space for students to be creative and compose their own music."

—Cami Tedoldi, Director of K-12 Music, Foxboro, MA Public Schools

"*Kids' Ukulele Songbook* is a fabulous introduction to the instrument and makes playing, singing, and creating songs easy for kids! Hands-on fun for all!"

—Amanda Lippert, elementary music teacher, Honolulu, HI